Also by Ashea Goldson

When Torn Down is All You Know

The Lovechild

Joy Comes In The Morning

Count It All Joy

Let Joy Arise

Resurrecting The Real Me

Embrace
Poetic Expressions For Your Spouse

Ashea S. Goldson

GoldWrite Publishing
Atlanta New York

Embrace

GoldWrite Publishing

Atlanta   NewYork

Unless otherwise indicated, all scripture quotations are taken from the Holy Bible, Old and New Testaments, King James version Thomas Nelson Publishers Nashville 1989

Book cover design by Anais Owens

Photo credit:Dreamstime.com/Cihan Demirok

Printed in The United States of America

<u>Dedication</u>

This book is dedicated to my Beloved Savior,

Jesus Christ

who taught me what real love is.

My Beloved is mine,
and I am his:he feedeth
among the lillies."

Song of Solomon 2:16

TABLE OF CONTENTS

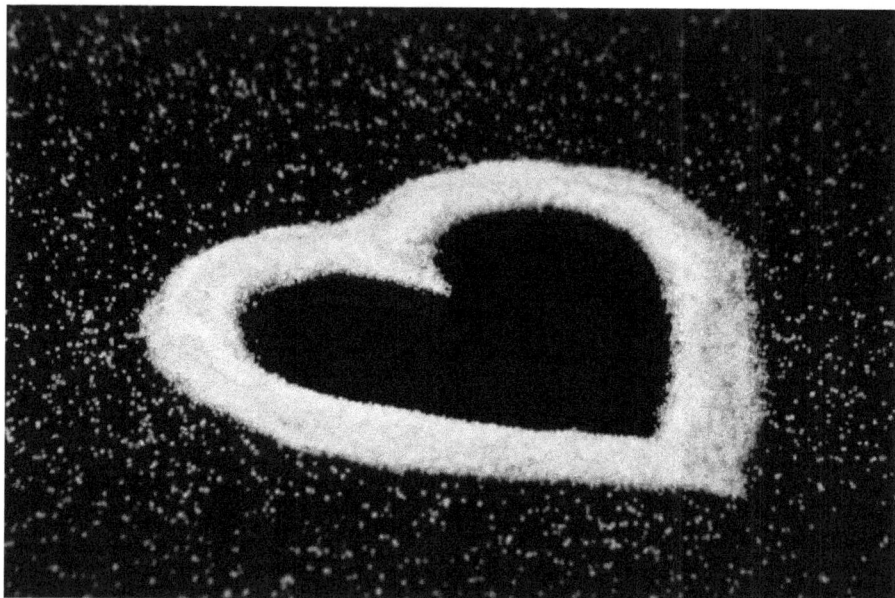

ACKNOWLEDGMENTS

To my husband of twenty five and a half years, Donovan,

with whom I've merged to express my love in the earth,

&

To the descendents of this love,

Anais and Safiya

To all the people who showed love by helping to make this book
happen, with encouraging words, actions or contributions to its
success or mine in any way,

I thank you.

INTRODUCTION

What is this thing called love and why must we embrace it?

Before we talk about love, let's first define the word embrace. According to the Merriam- Webster Dictionary, to embrace is to clasp in the arms, to encircle, to take up, to adopt or include, to encircle with the arms, or to embody.

Like the embrace, real love is an inclusive embodiment, an encircling of selflessness which can only come from God because He is love. It is not one-sided, emotional, ever changing, so-called love, characterized by infatuation and/or lust. Real love is pure, all en-compassing and all conquering.

Contrary to popular opinion, marriage is not just a legally binding contractual agreement. It is a *love* covenant, a sacred union between a man, a woman, and the Almighty God. Genesis 2:24 says, Genesis 2:24 says, "Therefore shall a man leave his father and his mother, and shall cleave unto his wife: and they shall be one flesh."

Created to imitate Jesus' relationship with the church, God ordained the institution of marriage to reflect the "agape" or unconditional love which Christ has for us. Marriage, although it should be romantic as well, is spiritual, not merely fleshy and temporal. Each spouse should minister perfect love to the other. It should then filter down to the children of the union and filter out to the community at large as the universal family is an essential part of the divine plan.

I have been married for over twenty five years and have had many ups and downs. However, I personally found out what "agape" love was as I experienced challenges throughout my life, devastating enough to rock the very foundations of my faith.Yet each time God I stumbled God covered and restored me. So I learned from the Master what it means to give real, selfless, forgiving, perfect love and thankfully, I learned what it means to receive it.

What can separate you from the love of God? Nothing. He is the great restorer. So trust him to do even what seems impossible in your marriage, in all of your relationships, and in your life as a whole. No matter what satanic interferences try to impede God's plan, trust what the Word says. So embrace the Savior, draw near to him, and His *manifested love* will bring you into victory.

Love covereth all things.

Proverbs 10:12

Ecstasy is what you make me feel.

Massaging every inch of me; my nerves stand on end.

Breathing your love filled air; I inhale your passion.

Releasing every desire aloud; I scream your name.

Absorbing the natural rhythm of us; I'm lost without you.

Captivating all of my senses. I'm filled with your essence.

Eternity is never enough.

What Love is

Love knows no obstacles,

No boundaries,

no limits

or constraints.

It is neither bribery

Nor is it held for ransom.

Promises

When you speak Promises
I catch the words
Rolling from your tongue
Lingering in your breath
Released into my inner ear
Tingling my ear lobes

As sweet lips
Brush against my cheek
Whispering love notes
Spraying sweet kisses
As the bridge of your nose
 Nuzzles the nape of my neck
With every nerve standing at attention

Your eyes a sleepy sea of memories
Fingertips touching warm shoulders
Light meeting darkness
Now with forever
And my body shivers
As my mind recalls
Promises of rapture
Fulfilled promises

Called into existence with your words

<u>Your Mark is On Me</u>

Your mark is on me
I can't wash it away
The oneness
Natural as it seems
A mystery to me
Embedded in my dreams.
We're connected now
And always communicating
By voicemail
By e-mail
By plane and by rail

Your mark is on me
We're linked by love
In heart and mind
No one is blind

Your mark on me
I follow you
I have no shame
I wear your ring
I took your name

Your mark is on me
You have the same
We're joined together

One flesh forever
Till death do us part

Your mark is on me.

On The Shore

When we lie
On the shore
The waves shall
Cleanse us
In our rest
From all day
Imprinting ourselves
In the sand

Lazy Day Love

A mist settles on my love,
A lazy day kind of love,
a thick honey-sweet
kind of love
forever finding solace
in the quiet
kind of love,
your aroma
seeping through my pores
like lemon in lemon meringue
it's the midnight tapping of my foot
to the rhythm of life's flow,
it's the curve of your hands,
making restraint
a mockery.
A mist settles on this lazy day love,
Promising no more
Than one wanton glance at a time,
Every time I celebrate you

<u>Daybreak Comes Quietly</u>

Daybreak comes quietly

Over the rugged hill

Softly, gently

Making time stand still

To be in your arms

How wonderful is the place

To embrace your love

To find pleasure in your face

Daybreak comes quickly

Over the rugged land

Softly, gently

making our love grand

Soulmate

My Soulmate

My partner for life

What is between us

But love

Love enticing

Love sufficing

Soulmate

My partner for life

Sing This Song

I sing this song

And it has your name in it

All the melody

Expresses your

Redundant rhythm

It is our song

And it plays forward

In my heart

Running towards eternity

When I'm awake

And backwards in my dreams

Leaving behind residual love

Every note

Screaming with the urgency

of this music we make

<u>Under The Oak Tree</u>

Under the oak tree

we sit laughing,

finishing each others sentences,

dreaming in each other's arms

holding hands

recalling memories

and making new ones

Loyalty

On good days

You become

For me

What I've always needed

In a mate

A loyal friend

But on bad days

That's when I'm the most grateful

That you're not only

still around

But still

Approachable.

Leaving You Behind

I found you looking
Outside the window
For me
But I was already
on my way
To work
 didn't want to wake you
From what seemed to be
 most peaceful sleep
But then
 your handprints
made their way
 to the window pane
And I looked up
to see the mist
Of tears
So good to be missed when I'm gone.

Forever

Forever is only a long time

Without you

Never final

Or lengthy

When I'm with you

It's greedy,

Wanting more time

Forever is a gift

When you're in my plans

Daily

When the scope of us

Is far reaching

Infinite

Hungry

And forever is only a long time

Without you.

<u>The Awe</u>

I float helplessly
with your reflection
rippling in the stream.
I lay cozy in the light
of your being
sleeping
through this perfect dream.
I wait for the awe
which is awesome
and when it comes upon me
in pieces
I am made whole
by the other half of me
which is you.

Overwhelmed

Oh,

When I look

Into your eyes

So rare

For fear of melting
Into one

Surrendering puddle

Of overwhelmed me

The Consummation

On our wedding day,

You and I

Can have

A little aloneness peace

And make waves

diligently

In the privacy

Of destinies fulfilled

Your Mystery

Your euphony rings

In my ears

A gentle humming

Until summer fades

Your posture

Eminates a radiance

An undeniable presence

I whisper at the calm

That is you

I'm forever fascinated

Forever in love with you

Your Lips

Your lips,
The most tender flesh
On your face
I could melt between them
Your lips
Like rose petals
Sweetly unplucked
In its fragrance
Like melons
Ripe with freshness
On a summer morning
Moist like the dew
Upon the crisp green
At dawn
Your lips
Warm like the sunshine
Leading me back to you
Each day.

EMBRACE

<u>Your Love Is Like Music</u>

Your love is like a sweet melody
Play another song for me

Music to my longing ears
Making joyful tears

A rhapsody to my hungry soul
I'm hypnotized in your hold

The harmony of your swaying
Each tender note playing

Perfectly in time
You're the rhythm to my rhyme

Each impression lingering
Every nerve is tingling

In my inner ear
Making joyful tears

Your slow beat moves in my spirit
You call and only I can hear it

Your love is like music

The Hands of Time

My love,
I find
The hands of time
Carving you
Like an undone sculpture
Finely etched
In gold
And diamonds
Your preciousness
Proven
Rejuvenated daily
I find
The hands of time
Finishing you
As an artist
Speaks beauty
Into a work
The hands of time
Confirming a masterpiece

The Wedding Day

"I do" she said
then turned her head
and kissed me
for all the church to see
We're now pronounced husband and wife
She'll share my life.

I take her hand
And walk up the aisle
And smile
We wave to our family
And friends
But that's not how it ends

Well wishers and people passing by
see us in our limo
And say goodbye
To the honeymoon we go
Where the unknown
I'll soon know
And we'll relish all that has been done
We've become one.

Stolen

You've stolen
A place in my heart
Surrounded me
With chemistry
You've taken me
On a journey
I've sailed before
But never for love
You're more
Than the finite space
I thought I owned.
You made your way
Into my world,
made logic
Into insanity
And all the while
You saved a place
In your heart
For me.

My Treasure

I searched for treasure

You filled me up

With laughter

And love

Your sparkling eyes

Bright as emeralds

Your lips red as rubies

Your hair

Dark as onyx

Your skin

Shining like diamonds

I find fortune at your feet

Beyond Comprehension Love

I love you with a beginning love

A call your own shots,

to the point,

Pull no punches,

Cut no corners

Down to the wire love

I love you with an endless love

An all consuming

incomprehensible love.

I love you with an almighty love

All covering

Ever merciful

Soul healing

Always forgiving

Essence of God

Who is love

And what love is.

with what has been given to me

mercy,

faith,

honor,

power,

strength

I shower you with the love that is me

and is in me

and flows from eternity

through me

a love beyond comprehension.

Your Scarf

I find your scarf
A single reminder
Of a snow covered day
the freshness of it
Stiffness the senses
A violet scarf
Comforting the nape
Of your neck,
Cradling the perfect oval
Of your head
A simple scarf
Draping your smooth skin
From the fierce wind
Soft lambswool
Clinging to the round
Of your shoulders
Falling down
To the small of your back
A simple cloth
Warming you
On a wintry day
Succumbing to your style
and elegance
A simple scarf
But not too simple
To be admired

Wedded Love is More

It's the whimsical dancing
Of spouses whose feet haven't hit the floor
It's washing dishes, burping babies
And other familiar chores
It's heart and mind, and body
It's so much more

Than the world would have us hold true
It's chocolate kisses,
and long stemmed roses,
it's everyday backrubs,
and a burned meal or two,

it's mortgages, bills and budgeting
sacrifice
and paying off the wedding ring

Silent empathy,
and strongly worded talks,
it's cold feet and late night walks.

It's more than passion's might
magical moments
Or an intense kiss goodnight.

It's retirement and growing together
It's sunny days and stormy weather.

It's all of these things for sure
Wedded love is so pure.

It commits and casts aside
all selfishness and foolish pride.
It makes sense of the nonsense,

stabilizes the condition,
brings pre-marital dreams into fruition.

Wedded love is
more than temporary gladness
It brings calm to a world
marked by madness.

<u>My Queen</u>

I keep you in high esteem

I'm your king

And you're my queen

You're like royalty

I'll shower you with gifts

Of love and loyalty

I could never show you enough

Of what I have inside

I want you to ride

This wave of eternity

And never be cross with me.

It would break my heart

To ever be apart

From the other half of my team.

I'm your coffee and you're my cream

You're my queen.

The Fragrance

It is strong

It is sweet

Like when honeymooners meet

To consummate this union

So new

And to breath in love's

Sweet perfume

Golden Anniversary

We've raised our kids

We did it well

Now we've so many

Good stories to tell

We've done our work

And we've run our race

Now it's time to take our place

In history

Fulfillment has come

Our dreams can now be.

__By The Fire__

Basking in the exquisiteness

Of your desire

                         I lye and wait

By the heat of the fire

In this secluded cabin

I find

                         I can unwind

Where spiral dreams

Do flow

To places

                         I've never dared to go.

The Honeymooners

The honeymooners

Drowning in the turbulence

Of whispered promises

Drunk with the taste of your skin

Feeling neither daylight

Nor nightfall

Letting nothing from outside in

Helpless like a foundling

I fall prey

To all that love reveals today

More than I could have fathomed

In a lifetime

You are the rhythm to my rhyme

On The Slopes

On the slopes
At every dawn and
Every sunset
I'm reminded of how we met
Out before the fields aglow
Of sunshine
Brightening the snow
Your gentle guiding hands
Helping me
When I could not stand
On skis,
on legs
You were too much for me
What I felt
Was more than gravity
Sailing down the slope
I concealed my hope
That you would be waiting
At the foot of the hill
And loving me still.

Your Arms

Your arms, any day

Unfolding to joy

Lye and rest

Wait to touch

Feel your arms

Unfolding any day

With the rain

hitting the glass

outside.

Ecstasy

I nuzzle

 in your existence

I am content.

I cuddle

 in your surrender

And flow backwards

 into infinity.

I invite myself

Into the depths of your longing

And find ecstasy

 abounding.

My Fisherman

A while ago
I looked across
A shallow pond
And saw you fishing
In such a gentle way,
And I wondered
What perhaps
If anything
Was going through your mind
What possessed you
A man of gallance
To take such pleasure
In the mundane horror
Of stabbing a fish
With a certain hook
Then I thought
Why not?
You certainly hooked me
One awesome creature
Conquering another

The Circle

The ring I wear

Is a circle of love

That endless circle is our love

It doesn't end though

Instead it flows around

And around.

It stays the same.

There is no up or down

It reminds me

Of what I'm committed to

And that I am only

Half without you

Silky Hands

The feel of your hands

Are like warm silk to me

I hold your body close

And taste the air you breathe

I find myself in a dream

When love professes

Its promise to me

I hold you

And next to you

I stand

And marvel at the warmth

Of your silky hands.

The Connection

My love

I'm full every morning

At the dining table

When I gaze into

What is lost to others,

Your true eyes

The connection

Between souls

And again

Become whole.

The Phonecall

I'm curled up here alone
Anxiously waiting to hear the phone
And when you ring
A melody I'll sing
I'll know your voice
I'll have no choice
I've been captured by it
In my dreams
And when I'm awake
How it seems
So very deep
And sensitive
Surely it will not let me live
We talk
and the roll of your tongue
soothes me
I'm greedy
To hear you
Again and again
Helplessly remembering
The where and the when
I've seen you in the sunlight
I press my ear to the receiver
So tight
And hang on to the notes
Of your voice all night.

Imagine

Being

With you creates in me

 Images of us

together

Surpassing reality

And all the while

In the quiet

 I imagine

I am quietly together with you.

Timeless

I never hesitate
To mark our relationship
Timeless
Always in
And never ending
Timeless
Endurance tested
And sweet thoughts sending
Timeless
As if a dream could make it more
As if reality could make it less
Timeless
Our own motionless phenomena
Conquering the elements
Of you plus me
Positioning ourselves in space,
in time,
timeless.

A Goodbye Kiss

A final Kiss

For we must part

Alas the dagger

In my heart

Fleeting moments

But a few

Must last until

The day anew

Wretched hints

Of love amiss

Must be treasured

Until love's

Next kiss

<u>Husband Away</u>

It has been too long

With you away

Missing the deep hands

Too late kisses

And half- smiles

Been too long

Since your knowing all eyes

And telling none lips

Have had an agenda

Cookie Dough Love

Our love is kneaded in its yearning

Rolled in its commitment

Stretched in its flexibility

Shaped in its creativity

And baked at the right temperature

With its passion.

Then cooled

and served in humility.

<u>Never Meant For Another</u>

Your strong arms
Never meant for another
Only for me
Holding me tight
Drowning In fluid ecstasy

Your sweet lips
Never meant for another
Only for mine
Surviving the test of time.

Your yielding body
Never meant for another
Only for my touch
I squeeze your firm flesh
And I want you so much

Your eyes
Never longing for another
They're mirrors into our world
And all we have is each other

<u>Now I know Love</u>

Now I know love
Thought I knew it before
Didn't know God could restore
    Like he did
Put the pieces
In place
Formed them gently
Not in haste
    Now I know love
Thought love was just romance
A quiet gaze
And a slow dance
Didn't know the enemy
Knew more about love
than me
    Funny

He knew if he could separate me from this power,

from the love of God

Then he could devour

What God intended

Didn't know I could be mended

    But I could

The enemy thought if he could stop me

Somehow try to block me

Persuade me his lies were real

Then he could control the way I feel,

    But he couldn't
Though satan tried to enslave me,

close my eyes to all God gave me,
the Holy Ghost ,
forever present
wouldn't let me go,
held me and shook me so I would know.
      And I did know
He'd never ever give up on me
His truth had already set me free.
Now I know what true love is supposed to be
      And it is
From the depths of the darkest hour
Love gives you the greatest power.
I've lived it,
proved it
      And now I know love.

Submit

It was already an intense evening as Norie smiled at her new in laws. Sitting around the dining room table with her husband Neil as her sister-in-law, Donna and her brother-in-law, Michael bickered back and forth about their children was not exactly her idea of entertainment. Donna and Michael were seated at opposite ends of the table and their two children, Michael Jr. and Sarah, were seated directly across from Norie and her husband, Neil.

Donna and Michael were what Donna considered a power couple, married for ten years, good looking, still in love with each other and still in love with their careers. They drove the latest cars, ate in expensive restaurants, and traveled extensively for their jobs. Their home, an immaculate, three story colonial, was like a palace with its perfectly maintained lawn and columned exterior and its huge twelve room interior.

Norie admired everything about them except for the way they raised their children. She tried not to judge them but she did not necessarily agree with all of their domestic

choices either.

Sarah hit Michael Jr. in the eye and took off running from the table.   "You're stupid."

"Don't call me stupid, big head. I'll get you." Michael Jr. ran behind her, nearly pulling down the entire tablecloth.

"Sarah and Junior stop acting like you've lost your minds." Donna stood up. "Come back here right now."

Neither of the children responded to their parent's pleading, but proceeded to stick out their tongues at each other.

"It's okay, I've got them." Michael excused himself from the table and followed the children.

"Parenthood is no picnic in the park, huh?" Norie noticed the wrinkles in Donna's forehead.

"Not with my schedule it's not. The daycare hours aren't long enough so I find myself rushing everyday and my weekend babysitter just quit yesterday." Donna put her hand on her forehead.

"Sounds a little hectic," Norie said.

"You could say that." Donna reached over to get a roll. "It's just not easy when you're trying to get everything done at home and trying to work at the same time."

"I can only imagine." Norie's voice was sympathetic.

Michael entered the room and took his seat. "That's why we've been looking for a nanny."

"Yes, but good ones are also hard to find," Donna said.

Michael looked directly at Norie and Neil. "How do you two plan to handle it when you have your kids?"

Suddenly, everyone in the room was quiet. The question was launched and there was no taking it back. Norie looked up from her meal to hear her husband's answer. They had only been married two months and the subject had not come up yet.

"My wife won't work when we have our kids." Neil dipped a spoon into the bowl of potatoes so matter of factly, Norie could not believe her ears.

Norie's fork dropped as well as her smile. Needless to say she was stunned at Neil's adamant attitude. Within seconds, the course of her life had changed forever. Her eyes filled up with tears as the one she loved betrayed her with his words. She couldn't believe that after only two months of marriage, she was already at a crossroad.

They always agreed that they would have children and they even agreed that they would wait for at least a year, if possible, before having them. However, they never discussed what would happen to their lives after the children were born.

Norie continued to eat as she tried to disguise her pain. She was too ashamed to contradict Neil in the presence of her in-laws. Yet she didn't know how she would be able to get through this family dinner. Norie sucked in all of her emotions and decided to wait for the appropriate time.

Back in the privacy of their two bedroom townhouse, Norie stepped out of the garden tub and dressed herself quickly. Neil came out of the shower and seemed to glare at her as she moved. He sat next to her on the bed and began to massage her shoulders. She hoped that he wouldn't make any advances toward her until she had a chance to express herself but they were newlyweds and Neil always had a healthy libido.

Norie took a deep breath. "What did you mean by telling your sister I can't work when we have our kids?"

"I mean that my wife is going to be a real mother, not a part-time one." Neil kept rubbing her shoulders.

"Are you accusing your own sister of not mothering her children?" Norie pulled away from Neil and began to rub her skin with apricot lotion.

"No, I'm not saying that," Neil replied.

"Then what are you saying?"

"I'm just saying I wouldn't choose that kind of life for my kids." Neil squinted his chestnut brown eyes and Norie knew that he was serious.

"Oh? What kind of life is that? "

"You know what I mean."

"No, I don't. She cares very much for her children and does the best she can for them."

"The best she can under the circumstances." Neil did not even blink.

"Circumstances?" Norie stood up and placed one hand on her hip.

"Yes, despite her career problems."

"Career problems? She's an acquisitions editor for a major publication and she's very good at it. I admire her. That doesn't sound like a *career problem*."

"Her career *is* her problem," Neil

said.

Norie knitted her eyebrows together. "What's wrong with that?"

Neil chuckled."With what?"

"With a woman having a career?"

"Absolutely nothing, in its place,"Neil said.

"In its place?"

"Yes, in its place." Neil's voice sounded harsher than usual.

"Okay, Mr. Know Everything, what place is that?"

"I may not know everything but I know that a career's place does not come before the kids," Neil continued.

"That's so unfair." Norie felt her eyes filling up with tears again.

Neil cleared his throat."I just don't believe a mother can have a successful family life at the same time she's out chasing her own ambitions."

Norie sniffled."What about my career, Neil?"

"What about it?"

"What about all I've worked so hard for my MBA and everything? I've been working at the bank for two years and I love my job. I love everything about it."

"I know. I'm not asking you to give it up permanently, just to postpone it for a while."

"A while?" Norie stood up and put her hands on her round hips.

"Just until the children are old enough."

"Old enough to do what? Drive?"

Neil chuckled. "So funny."

"Somehow it doesn't seem fair to have to put my life on hold indefinitely while you give up nothing." Norie couldn't hold the tears in any longer.

"I'll be giving too." Neil touched her face and wiped a tear away with his finger.

"Giving what?"

"Giving you and the kids everything you need, money, love and support, everything."

"But what about my identity?" Norie fell across the bed, pouting.

"You have one. You're Mrs. Norie Walker." Neil sat down next to her and began to stroke her wavy hair.

"I can see this is going nowhere," Norie whined.

"I'm sorry I upset you. Listen, we're both tired so let's talk in the morning. Everything will work out just fine." Neil pulled her close and aimed his lips at hers but Norie turned away.

Neil said a quick prayer and jumped into bed.

She faked a smile and slid under the covers. Her heart was still racing and her cheeks were still warm with frustration. She felt his arm around her as she drifted off to sleep. *Lord, please help me to get through this.*

Norie woke up to a new day. Everything was fresh - her new linen, her new job, and her marriage. She could hear the sound of birds singing outside her open window. She walked over and touched the glass, leaving faint fingerprints upon the windowpane. The smell of strawberry pancakes floated in from the kitchen and filled the room.

She remembered the argument she and her husband had the night before. It was their first real one since they were married, and although they vowed they would never go to bed angry, Norie found herself a little less forgiving than she expected. After all Neil apologized and promised they would work things out. Still, she couldn't get their disagreement out of her mind.

Why is he being so stubborn and why did his sister have to start rambling on about her domestic challenges anyway?

Norie decided to consult God about the issue. She got down on her knees and wept until there were neither tears nor words left in her.

"Lord, I know you've made us one. Help me to understand my husband and help him to understand me. I want what you want for our family, Lord, so therefore I submit to your will, in Jesus' name. Amen."

Norie felt a sense of peace. By the time she got off of her knees, Neil was serving her breakfast in bed. Deep inside she knew that everything would work out, even though she wasn't sure how. She reminded herself of the wedding vows they recited just two months ago, their covenant with each other and with the Lord.

Tasting the syrup on Neil's lips, she lost herself in his kisses. She enjoyed her husband and decided to deal with the issue of children when the time came.

"Norie, I love you and I only want what is best for us and our future." Neil reached for Norie's hand.

"So do I," Norie agreed.

"I want to make wise choices."

"I trust you Neil but more importantly, I trust God." She put her hands in his and had no doubts.

"He won't let us down." He kissed her forehead.

If you haven't received Jesus as your personal

savior, do it today because God is love.

EMBRACE

www.ingramcontent.com/pod-product-compliance
Lightning Source LLC
Chambersburg PA
CBHW071844020426
42331CB00007B/1846